Modern Christian Martyrs

Deslee Campbell

Memorable Christians: Book 6

Dedicated to my mother-in-law's friend,
Sister May Hayman and her fiancé,
Rev. Vivian Redlich
and the other 331 martyrs of New Guinea

Table of Contents

Prologue

Prologue

May their names be remembered and their deeds celebrated on this earth: yet how easily we forget them. The Early Church celebrated and remembered its martyrs: those who proved that they could overcome the evil of this world, just as their Master had done. They became the immortals: Peter, Paul, James, Justin Martyr, Polycarp, Agnes, Perpetua and Felicity and so many more, who were often depicted holding the crown of martyrdom they had earned.

The modern women and men from many nations noted below are "a great cloud of witness" and will be listed according to the date of their martyrdom as that is the aspect of their lives that is the major concern of this survey.

Unfortunately the martyrdom of Christian nationals, missionaries and Western Christian aid workers remains a problem: even for neutral, secular organizations such as the Red Cross and Medicines Sans Frontiers. The greatest number of deaths occurred in the 1970's when, on average, 377,000 Christians died as martyrs each year. The average fell as low as c.160,000 in 2000 and to 90,000 in 2017 but it is anticipated that the number will rise by 2025 to 100,000 or more. This may be because of rise in ultra-nationalism (such as in Myanmar/Burma and China) or because of militant Islamic activity: although, because ISIS has been defeated in Syria and Iraq, crucifixions and beheadings may decline. While missionary work (especially for women and children) used to be dangerous because medical care was lacking, the dangers now arise from terrorism, anarchy, war and state sponsored brutality.

Chapter 1
James Hannington (1847-1885)

James Hannington was born in Sussex in England into a well-off family which owned Hannington's Department Store. His father, Charles Smith Hannington, ran its hardware warehouse. Young James was educated by a private tutor but then attended Temple School in Brighton. He left school at the age of fifteen to work in with his father but, in 1864, he obtained a commission in the 1st Sussex Artillery Corps and eventually rose to the rank of major.[1]

Charles Smith Hannington had built a chapel on his property in 1852. The family was Congregationalist but became Church of England in 1867 and the chapel became a recognised Anglican placed of worship.

When two missionaries were killed near Lake Victoria in Africa in 1872 James, by then a married man, volunteered for missionary service with C.M.S. and went to St Mary's Hall, Oxford University, for training. He graduated with a Bachelor of Arts and was ordained deacon in 1974 and priest in 1875 and then served as a curate for some years. In 1882, he set out for Africa with six other missionaries and reached Zanzibar but illness forced him to return home. Before he left for the second time James Hannington was consecrated bishop 1884.

Plate 5.1. Bishop Hannington. Public domain.

In 1885, Bishop James Hannington was the first Anglican bishop to be appointed to Eastern Equatorial Africa, which included the Kingdom of Bugunda/Rwanda when he was thirty-seven years old. Christianity had been welcome in Uganda in the 1870's by King Mutesa of Bugunda but his insecure son, Mwanga II, (king from 1884) opposed all foreign presence in his lands. Christian writer Colin Reed provides a number of politico-cultic reasons for this opposition, but the issue of homosexual behaviours was probably paramount.[2] Alexander Mackay, a Presbyterian minister, wrote that Mwanga *"had copied homosexual behaviour from Arabs of his court"*.[3]

When Bishop Hannington, arrived at Lake Victoria he and his party were imprisoned at Kyando and tortured for eight days, during which the bishop recorded in his journal that he was singing "Safe in the Arms of Jesus". First the porters were killed and the following day (October 29, 1885) Hannington was speared to death by Chief Luba on the orders of King Mwanga II, who took the advice of his senior chiefs and seers.[4] The reasons were complex: a mixture of superstition, insecurity of a young, new king, hatred of Europeans and perhaps fear of the political or spiritual power that such a high-status European would embody and bring with him.

Many other Christians were martyred[5] both Roman Catholics and Anglicans, as widespread persecution of Christians followed.[6] King Mwanga's first native victim was his own senior advisor, Joseph Rugarma, a Roman Catholic, who was beheaded for criticising the king's debauchery and the killing of Bishop Hannington (in 1885). Three pages, Joseph Mukasa Blaikuddembe (d.1885), Mark Kakumba and Noah Serwanga were killed for refusing the homosexual demands of King Mwanga (who was a serial rapist).[7] These Christian pages were speared, hacked to pieces and/or burnt alive at Namugongo and two more were later speared at Paimol in Northern Uganda.

Altogether in 1885, 23 Anglican and 22 Catholic young men were murdered for their faith and because they also refused the king's homosexual demands. *"These included his headman, Charles Lwanga and a thirteen year old page, Kitzito"*.[8] (Those with European names had obviously been baptised). About two or three hundred minor chiefs and others were also killed (1885-87).[9]

The Catholic victims were canonised by Pope Paul VI in 1964[10] and he visited Uganda in July, 1969.[11] The Ugandan church has been built on the blood of its martyrs. Every year crowds throng to Kyando to see the stone on which the bishop's blood was shed and the cave that served as his library, pulpit, altar and bedroom and to drink water from the well from which the martyr drank,[12] although as a former Congregationalist Bishop Hannington might have been embarrassed by that if he had known.

Chapter 2
Marguerite Nalbandian (d.1915)

Marguerite Nalbandian was a young Armenian woman teacher who was a friend and fellow worker of the Scandinavian missionary Miss Bodil Björn, who worked as a missionary among the Armenian people in Turkey during World War I. It was Bodil who took the photograph in Plate 2.1.

"At that time the Christians were living in conditions of constant oppression and persecution".[13]

Many drawings, photographs and lithographs of massacres and persecutions of Armenians from as far back as the 17th century are extant.[14]

The photograph in Plate 2.1 shows one class of the 120 Armenian children who were enrolled in the school organised by the Scandinavian Women's Missionary Workers. The Armenia teacher, Margarid (also translated Marguerite) Nalbandian, in the middle of the class. They all were herded into a barn and burned to death. On the back of the photo Bodil Björn wrote:

"One of the classes in the day-school in Mush with their teacher Margarid... Margarid Nalbandian and most of the 120 children of the day-school were murdered in 1915".

**2.1. Marguerite Nalbandian's class of doomed children.
Mush, Turkey, 1915.[15]**

The Ottoman entity was a predominantly Islamic state in which religious minorities were second class citizens, or worse. It centred on Turkey, the capital of which was the ancient Byzantine capital of Constantinople (now Istanbul) that the Turks had conquered from the Greek-speaking Byzantine Christians in 1453. The Ottoman Empire's official, stated policy in 1915 was to rid the empire of all non-Muslims: Armenians, Greeks, Assyrians and others. The main architect of the policy was the Ottoman Minister of Interior, Talaat, who wrote:

"All Armenians, who are subjects of the Ottoman Empire, from five years of age or older, must be expelled from the city and destroyed".[16]

---

1. https://upload.wikimedia.org/wikipedia/commons/2/2e/
Skolepiker_fra_Musch_med_l%C3%A6rer_-_PA_0699_U_36_152.jpg

Coincidentally this expulsion began in Constantinople just as the first ANZAC troops were landing on the Gallipoli peninsular: April 25, 1915.

In 1915, Bodil Björn witnessed the murder of children in her care and of numerous teachers, assistants and Armenian priests, simply because they were Armenian Christians. Armenian children were killed by being thrown into the Euphrates River at Deir Zor where the Chief of Police, M. Sidqi, controlled operations; or thrown into lakes and the Black Sea.[17] The American ambassador to Turkey, Henry Morgenthau, reported that "*hundreds of children were stabbed by the Turks and thrown into the River Euphrates*".[18] Some children were stabbed and bayoneted, others were burnt alive or starved. Some were poisoned by Turkish doctors (such as Dr S. Ali, head of health services in Trabzon Province).[19] Some children did die of disease but the vast majority of the dead were deliberately slaughtered.

Armenians were particularly targeted because many of them lived near the Russian border and might prove dangerous as Turkey was at war with Russia and Russia was a Christian country with a large Armenian population. When the Bolsheviks deposed and killed the Czar and his family (as the next chapter will discuss) they withdrew Russia from the Great War and Armenians could no longer depend upon any Russian help or protection.

The tragedy concerning Marguerite Nalbandian and her pupils was part of the official policy of the Ottoman Empire. It is estimated that one and a half million Armenians were disposed of between April 1915 and Turkey's capitulation in 1918.

Not only did Bodil Björn leave photographs and a detailed diary but so did her fellow missionary, Maria Jacobsen, although they did not always work together and Bodil worked in three different countries. Maria's diary, which extended from 1907 to 1919, has recently been republished in English. The photograph of emaciated children in Plate 2.2 is from Maria's diary. Yet a third lady missionary has also provided eye-witness accounts which verify those harrowing events: Alma Johanason from Sweden, wrote '*A People in Exile: One Year in the Life of the Armenians*'. Similarly, Amy Atkinson, the wife of an American doctor, meticulously kept a daily diary, Part 2 of which has recently been published as '*The German, the Turk and the Devil made a Triple Alliance. Harpoot Diaries 1908-1917*.[20]

Many Armenian children were rescued by Bedouin families in the Syrian desert where they had been driven and then orphaned and many of them were converted to Islam. After the war a 'Rescue Committee of Armenia Orphans' was formed in Aleppo, Syria, to buy them from Arab and Kurdish tribes and also to collect the bones of Armenian martyrs for Christian burial and memorialisation.

Two movies have been made about Bodil Björn: '*They Call Me Mother*' (2006) and '*Map of Salvation*' (2015) but this chapter is about the martyr Marguerite Nalbandian. The Turks may not have liked the presence of European Christians but they did not deliberately kill them but most of the Europeans were traumatised by what they had witnessed in Turkey.

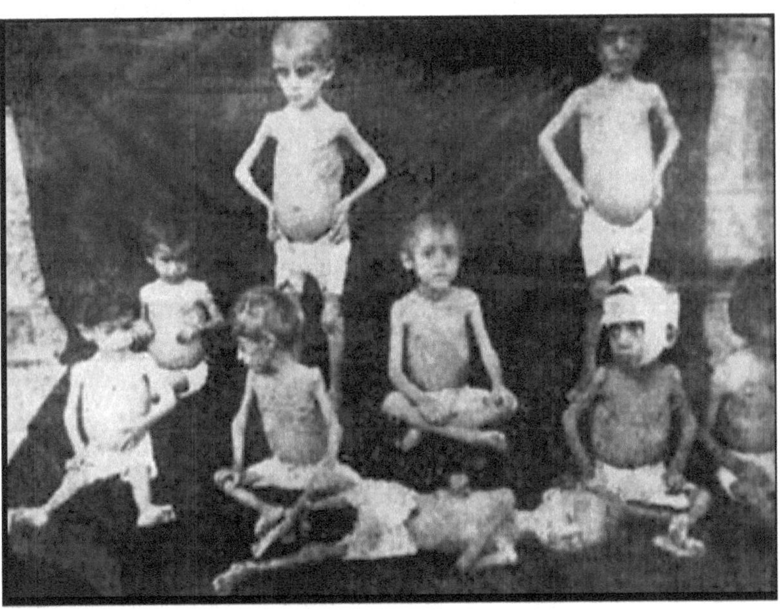

Plate 2.2. Starving children collected by the Committee of the Middle East, Kharput, Turkey. Photograph by Maria Jacobsen. Public domain.

Chapter 3
Elizabeth Fyodorovna (1864-1918)

Elizabeth (called Ella) was the daughter of Princess Alice, one of Queen Victoria's daughters, and Grand Duke Louis IV of Hesse. Her sister, Alexandra, was the last empress of Russia.

When Elizabeth was fourteen, in 1878, her mother and one sister died of diphtheria so that Elizabeth and her younger sister, Alexandra, spent time growing up in England with their grandmother, Queen Victoria, so that they became fluent speakers of English.[21] Her example in life was her paternal ancestor Elizabeth Thuringia of Hungary (1207-1231), another philanthropic and pious woman, who suffered early widowhood because of the Crusades and was also canonised (albeit by the Roman Catholic Church).[22]

In June 1884 Elizabeth married Grand Duke Sergei Alexandrovich, the fifth son of the Russian Emperor Alexander II and Princess Marie of Hesse-Dasrmstadt, a daughter of Queen Victoria, so that both Elizabeth and Sergei were grandchildren of Queen Victoria. Together this young couple adopted the Grand Duke Dmitri Pavlovitch and his older sister Grand Duchess Maria Pavlovna after their mother had died in childbirth.[23]

Being a German-English Princess, Elizabeth was a Protestant but in 1891, about six years after her marriage, she chose to receive the Holy Chrismation of the Russian Orthodox Church. Apparently Queen Victoria was sympathetic whereas other family members were upset; but Elizabeth said that she was following her conscience.[24] After her marriage into the Russian imperial family Elizabeth had engaged in intense study of Russian culture, religion and language which led her to the decision to both convert and to embrace Russia.

Elizabeth and Sergei lived in Moscow as he was the Governor-General of Moscow; while she devoted herself to philanthropic work and reluctantly participated in the frivolities of court life. Then they moved into the Nicholas Palace in the holy Kremlin. It was so near this home that the Grand Duke was

"

assassinated by a bomb on February 18, 1905, that the Grand Duchess was able to rush out into the snow and help gather the pieces of his dismembered body and to arrange for the Duke's wounded coachman to be taken to hospital where he died.[25]

Although she was devastated at the loss of her husband and cousin, Elizabeth visited the assassin, Ivan Kalyayev, a Social Revolutionary, in prison. She forgave him, gave him The Gospel and urged him to read it and to repent.

Elizabeth's life changed dramatically. She withdrew from the life of frivolity, gave away her jewellery and sold her luxurious possessions. She placed herself in obedience under the spiritual direction of the elders of the Zosima Hermitage and built a great tomb for her husband at the Chudov Monastery. She then left the palace and lived in two rooms in a house she obtained at Ordinka and opened the Martha and Mary Home in Moscow, which was dedicated to both the practical and the spiritual life. In this home she helped the poor and orphans and, in 1909, Elizabeth and seventeen others were dedicated as Sisters of Love and Mercy.

Many women joined the order, including some of the high born who were generally not as devout as other women so that, previously, they had not entered convents since the Byzantine Era. She was able to open a hospital, an orphanage, accommodation for messenger boys and girls, and to found churches and pursue other charitable work. *She radiated an inner light, especially by her love and tenderness*.[26] One Sister, Barbara, became her close and faithful companion.

Plate 3.1. Elizabeth, Saint and Martyr of the Russian Orthodox Church. Painting by Stepan Alexandrovsky, 1906. Public Domain.

The Grand Duke Sergei had been a particular patron of the Holy Land and was chairman of the Palestinian Society. During his lifetime they had visited the holy sites of Zion together and they had helped finance the construction of the Russian compound and dramatic Church of St Mary Magdalene on the Mount of Olives, built in memory of her mother-in-law, the Empress Maria Alexandrovna, by her children. Indeed, both Elizabeth and Sergei were present at its consecration.

Elizabeth's own experience as a pilgrim gave her a particular concern for pilgrims and she readily took over Sergei's chairmanship of the Society.[27]

When World War I broke out Russia's neighbour, Turkey, almost accidentally found itself on opposite sides of the conflict, fighting with Germany and Austria as the Triple Alliance. Russian casualties were high and Elizabeth devoted herself to treating sick and wounded soldiers including German soldiers (for which she was criticised and maligned) and she also visited troops at the front.[28]

When the Boshevik revolutionaries, who had overthrown the Russian government, inspected the Martha and Mary House at the end of 1917, they permitted it to continue functioning but Elizabeth was suddenly arrested during Easter of 1918. She was transported, first to Ekaterinburg and then to Alapaevsk, along with Sister Barbara, who refused to leave her, and six of her young male relatives: Grand Duke Serbi Michailovich and the Princes John, Igor, Constantiine and Vladimir, as well as Theodore Remez. On July 18, the Grand Duke was shot and the remainder were thrown down a well. Hand grenades were then thrown down because they did not die. Elizabeth tended their wounds and sang Old Russian hymns until they had all passed into Eternity. At much the same time her sister, Czarina Alexandra, with Czar Nicholas II, their four daughters (Princesses Tatiana, Olga, Maria and Anastasia) and the Crown Prince Alexei were shot to death.

When the White Army (non-Communists) recaptured the area the remains of Saint Elizabeth and the young grand dukes were found and eyewitness testimonies were recorded. Saint Elizabeth's relics were taken for safety to Beijing, China, and placed in the Church of St Seraphim of Sarov and eventually taken to lie in the Church of St Mary Magdalene on the Mount of Olives, the church which she and Grand Duke Sergi had helped to build, and, indeed, they were present at its consecration.

Later, in 1981 and then in 1992 (after the fall of Communist USSR) Elizabeth was glorified as a saint and a New Martyr of the Russian Orthodox Church. Her statue is one of the ten martyrs recently created for the West End portal of Westminster Abbey.[29]

Chapter 4
John Cornelius Stam (1907-1934)

John Cornelius Stam was born in Paterson, New Jersey, the seventh of ten children of a Dutch immigrant father, Peter Stam, and his wife, who had French Huguenot forebears, a family that was dedicated to social welfare through the Star of Hope Mission. John, a shy lad, gave his life to the Lord when he was fifteen and went on to study for a business diploma, meanwhile becoming an accomplished street evangelist.[30]

Betty Scott was raised in China by her missionary parents but returned to the U.S.A. to attend Wilson College in Pennsylvania, after which, in 1928, she enrolled in Moody Bible Institute. John Cornelius Stam enrolled the following year and they attended the same regular prayer meeting for China, which was conducted under the banner of the China Inland Mission (now the Overseas Missionary Fellowship).

Betty returned to China when her student days were over. For her it was home. She volunteered for an un-evangelised part of China and was accepted as a C.I.M. missionary in 1931.[31]

When Betty left for China she and John had 'an understanding' but C.I.M. required an engagement 'in country' of at least one year. As well as that, John had another year of study to complete and must be accepted by C.I.M., which was a challenge as he had to be called to China, not to Betty: and it's sometimes hard to separate the two.

Plate 4.1. Martyrs John and Betty Stam. Public domain.

John arrived in China in 1832 but they were not posted together. They were, however, married on October 25, 1933. Eleven months later Betty gave birth to baby Helen Priscilla[32] in the Methodist hospital in Wuhu. She was a beautiful child with blue eyes and curly hair.[33]

Upon their return to the remote, almost inaccessible, walled mountain city of Tsingteh they rented a shop-front on a flagstone street, which was both their home and their meeting room. This was a time of heightened nationalism and hatred of foreigners. Wild rumours were swirling around but the sudden arrival of a band of Communist bandits was unexpected and the Stams were trapped. When their home was overrun the invaders demanded ransom of $20,000. Betty had served them tea and cakes[34] but they took John away to the town's jail. Later they returned for Betty and baby Helen. Some reports say that they were imprisoned for a few days. Then the Stams were taken away: in their underwear.[35] Betty rode a horse with the baby but John walked, with his hands tied behind his back and they travelled 19km (12 miles) to another town.

John had managed to leave a note saying:

"My wife, baby and myself are today in the hands of the Communists in the city of Tsingteh. Their demand is $20,000 dollars for our release.

All our possessions and our stores are in their hands, but we praise God peace in our hearts and a meal tonight. God grant you wisdom in what you do, and us fortitude, courage, and peace of heart. He is able, - and a wonderful friend in such a time.

Things happened so quickly this A.M. They were in the city just a few hours after the ever-persistent rumors (sic) really became alarming, so that we could not prepare to leave in time. We were just too late.

The Lord bless and guide you, - and as for us,- may God be glorified whether by life or death.

In Him,

John C. Stam[36]

The family was thrust into an abandoned house for the night and John was tied to a heavy bedpost. Betty wrapped her baby in a sleeping bag and hid her among quilts with a letter, two diapers and a $5 or $10 note. Miraculously, Helen slept there silently for twenty-seven hours.

In the morning Betty and John were taken to a hillside. John's throat was cut and Betty's head was almost severed from the back. A Chinese local who protested, Anhui Miaosheo (born 8/12/1934) was also killed with them.[37] Betty and John were not yet thirty years of age.

An old woman whispered to Mr Lo Ke-chou, a lay evangelist, that a baby had been left in the deserted house. Mr Lo, a Mrs Wang and her son found the dead bodies and procured two coffins. They attempted to sew their heads back on and then wrapped them in clean white sheeting and covered them with 100 pounds of limestone each. The coffins had to be left on the hill until the danger had passed before they could be buried.

Meanwhile baby Helen Priscilla Stam (known as 'the miracle baby) had been found. Mr Lo was able to purchase Lactogen baby formula with the money Betty had left (a rare commodity) and his wife cared for Helen while they carried her and their son in a coolie's vegetable basket to the Methodist hospital in Wuhu where she had been born. Later she was taken to her maternal grandparents mission station in the North where Helen lived with them for five years. As they were growing old she was adopted by her mother's sister and her husband, George and Helen Mahy, and she took their family name. Because they were missionaries in the Philippines Helen grew up there but returned to the USA for college. She did not marry and worked as an editor for scientific journals.

Plate 4.2. Baby Helen Stam arriving with Mr Lo (left) and Mrs Lo (Centre right).

After his war-service in World War II, Betty's brother, Kenneth Scott, became a medical-missionary in Korea and India. He testified that a great many young people were inspired by the Stam's deaths and responded to the news by volunteering for missionary service.[38]

Chapter 6
Vivian Frederick Barnes Redlich (1905-1942)

Vivian Frederick Barnes Redlich was born in Natal, South Africa to Matilda LeMaitre (1875-1927) and Rev. Canon Edwin Basil Redlich (1878-1960). His mother was born on the Channel Islands in St Helier, Jersey, and his father had lived in India and the Channel Islands before they moved to Colonial South Africa. By 1942 Rev. Basil Redlich was rector of the village of Little Bowden in England. Both Rev and Mrs Redlich died in Leicestershire, England.

Vivian Redlich was ordained in 1932 in the Wakefield Diocese, England five years after his mother had passed away. He went to Australia to join the Brotherhood of St Andrew to work in rural and remote Queensland and was posted to Winton, which has recently been made famous by the discovery of well-preserved dinosaur bones, including previously unknown species.

After his five year term was completed Rev Redlich applied to the Australian Board of Missions to work in Papua New Guinea and was accepted and sent as priest-in-charge to the Sangara Mission Station thirty miles (c.40 km) inland from Gona Mission Station, which was on the North Coast of Papua.

Japan joined the Axis powers on 7/12/1941 during World War II in the belief that the German side would win, after which they would stand to gain territory in the Pacific region and expand their empire. They quickly captured Malaya, Singapore and Rabaul, New Britain. Despite the Japanese attack on the American fleet anchoring in Pearl Harbour, America remained Japan's strongest threat and therefore New Zealand and Australia had to be overcome but the long island of Papua-New Guinea, which had been an Australian protectorate since the end of World War I, stood in the way. In the mistaken belief that the jungle path (Kokoda Track) was a road, their plan was to land on the Northern Coast of Papua-New Guinea and fight their way over the Owen Stanley Ranges in order to conquer Port Moresby.

The Rt. Rev'd Bishop Philip strong had broadcast a message to the Anglican mission stations. His final words were:

"I cannot tell the future. I cannot guarantee that all will be well

- that we shall all come through unscathed. One thing only I can guarantee is that, if we do forsake Christ here in Papua in His Body the Church, He will not forsake us, He will uphold us, He will sustain us, He will strengthen us, and he will guide and keep us through the days that lie ahead... Let us trust and not be afraid".[39]

The Japanese found the conquest of PNG a difficult task and the casualties were very heavy but they advanced through the mountains until their supplies were exhausted. As the Allied forces retreated they reached supply depots but left nothing behind, whereas the Japanese carried ammunition but not supplies. The Allies made a stand to hold Imita Ridge above Port Moresby on September 15/ 16, 1942, after which the starving Japanese advanced to the rear.

One missionary who survived the war was Rev. R. L. Newman, who had worked in Eroro for nine years and who, with his wife, was hidden in a cave in the hills and fed by local people. Another was Anglican cleric Rev. Benson who surrendered to the Japanese and finished up living in a Roman Catholic lepers' colony.

For the staff at Sangara and Isivita there was no such help. Rev. Vivian Redlich, Sister Margery Brenchley, Miss Lilla Lashmar, Rev. Henry Holland, Mr John Duffill and a six year old boy had been betrayed, captured and beheaded. Their bodies were never recovered, apparently cast into the sea.[40]

Rev. Vivian Redlich and his beautiful fiancée, Sister May Hayman, died within a day or so of each other but not together, nor can they lie in peace together as Vivian's resting place will never be known.

Plate 5.1. Vivian Redlich. Public domain.

An Australian War Crimes Tribunal tracked the executioner (Komai, a Japanese Sub-Lieutenant) who was already dead. Five (or perhaps seven) renegade local men were later hanged for betraying missionaries to the Japanese. Rev. Newman, who attended the executions, heard their confessions.

After the war the martyrs' cathedral was built in Dogura as their memorial and as the centre of Anglican work and education in PNG.

Chapter 6
May Hayman (1906-1942)

May Hayman was born on 30/1/1906 to Marian Turner (1965-1928) and Francis Edward Hayman (1853-1920) in Adelaide, South Australia. The family was South Australian but mother and daughter moved to Canberra, the new Commonwealth capital city, where May worked with her brother-in-law in an office of the Department of Interior. Having decided to become a nurse, May returned to Adelaide for her training.[41]

Plate 6.1, May Hayman at 25. Public domain.

As a nursing sister May Hayman worked at Dubbo Base Hospital in N.S.W. and attended Holy Trinity Anglican Church,[42] before securing a position at Canberra Community Hospital where she could be with family members. In 1949, May was memorialised in St John's Church, Reid, in Canberra, with a stained-glass window.[43] She was described as having sparkling eyes and beautiful golden hair.

In 1936, having gained some years of clinical experience May went with the Australian Board of Missions to Gona, on the North Coast of Papua, where she met Rev. Vivian Redlich, an English clergyman who ran the Anglican mission base at nearby Sangara. She would later accept his marriage proposal.

On 21/7/1942, Japanese forces landed at Gona Beach. The women at the Anglican Mission station of Gona and their house-boys actually watched a naval battle taking place. They had been told by their bishop to retreat to Isivita Mission, which was a 38 mile walk if they did not get lost in the jungle. They reached Siai and felt safe but were totally isolated for three weeks.[44]

Rev. Benson decided to try to break out and he survived the war by voluntarily surrendering to the Japanese. Sister May Hayman and Miss Mavis Parkinson were betrayed to the Japanese and bayoneted to death on or around August 12, 1942, with Lucian, who tried to protect them and whose story is told in Chapter 7. Their remains were found by Australian troops the following February and they were buried at Sangara Mission station on 26th February, 1943.

April 19, 1943 and those stationed at Isivita Mission, Rev. Henry Holland and Mr John Duffill, were beheaded on the beach with those from Sangara Mission.

They were among the first of 333 Christian workers of various denominations brutally killed by the Japanese invaders of New Guinea. After the war ten bamboo crosses representing penitence were sent from Japan to the Anglican Archbishop of Brisbane via Rev. Frank Coaldrake, an avowed pacifist and a missionary in Japan from 1947 and who became Chairman of the Australian Board of Missions.

In May, 1943, Bishop Philip Strong went to Sangara to restart the Anglican work there. He returned in December of that year to find a newly built church and a functioning congregation led by a local man, Vernon. The font of beaten copper, which had been made by Rev. Redlich, was still in use. At the East end two windows had been inserted in the wall. They had been taken from the bombed out mission house, from the bedrooms previously occupied by the martyrs Margery Benchley and Lilla Lashmar who had seen the sun shining in every morning. For the community they were a symbol of the Gospel light the martyrs had brought to them.

In 1945 the bishop came on a pilgrimage to the resting placers of his priests and lay-workers and eyewitness. As he came to the graves of May Hayman and Mavis Parkinson an eye-witness recorded that:

"No sooner had the Bishop set his feet upon the ground that, with hat removed and the sorrow of his heart fully revealed in his face and posture, he made his way to the graves and there prostrated as before an altar, his inmost soul laid bare before his God. Such a moment is not to be told in words of earthly origin, but all present found themselves upon their knees, even the driver of the American vehicle whose background in spiritual matters is not known. The silence was barely broken until Even-song was said, joined in by the natives who had gathered at the approach of their bishop. Three Australian signallers and a native, named Christian, who were present at the burial, took part in these and following services. Christian had played an important part in the recovery of the missionaries bodies, and his faithfulness cannot be over-estimated". [45]

Chapter 7
Lucian Tapiedi (c.1921-1942)

Lucian Tapiedi was born in about 1921 in Taupota village in the Milne Bay district of North Papua. It is believed that his father was a sorcerer. Lucian was educated at Anglican mission schools where he came under the influence of Nita Inman, a schoolteacher, and Rev. Edwin Nuagoro, an indigenous priest.[46]

For two years (1939-1940) Lucian was trained to be a teacher at St Aidan's Teacher Training College, at Dogura, and he became a teacher and evangelist at the Sangara Mission Station in 1941 when Rev. Vivian Redlich was in charge.

Plate 7.1. Lucian Tapiedy's statue,
Westminster Abbey. Wikipics.

On January 4, 1942 the Japanese military invaded Papua and the ten staff members at Sangara tried to evade capture and escaped to a village of the Onokaiva people. One of the villagers, Hivijapa by name, cut Lucian's young life short by hacking him to death with an axe. Two women missionaries were beheaded by the Japanese the next day.[47]

Lucian's body was retrieved by a man named Christian who buried him near the two women missionaries, May Hayman and Mavis Parkinson, whom Lucian had died trying to protect. When the bishop visited the graves of Sister May Hayman and Miss Mavis Parkinson, as recounted in the previous chapter, he consecrated the gravesites, which were surrounded by a fence. A young boy kept saying "Lucian, Lician" and appeared distressed. He was indicating that the martyr Lucian's grave was outside the fence and therefore his grave had not been consecrated. Once this was understood the fence was moved and the appropriate rites were performed.

The murderer, Hivijapa, later became a Christian, adopted Lucian's name and built a church in his memory. That church was destroyed by an eruption of Mount Lamington in 1951 but was rebuilt at Popondetta. Another memorial church, St Lucian's Six Mile, was built in Port Moresby, but Lucian is buried at Sangara.[48]

All of the martyrs of Papua-New Guinea are commemorated each year on September 2 and a statue of Lucian, by Tim Crawley, has been placed (with nine other modern martyrs) above the Great West Door of Westminster Abbey, the church in which the monarchs of Britain are married and the champions and heroes of Britain and the Empire have, for hundreds of years, been buried.

Chapter 8
Irene Stefani "Nyaatha" (1891-1930)

Sister Irene was born Aurelia Jacoba Mercede Stefani on August 22, 1891 in the small village of near Brescia, Italy, the oldest of four children. She was confirmed at the age of seven. Her mother died when Aurelia was sixteen years old and she helped her father raise her sisters, Marietta and Antonietta, and her brother Ugo, who died at a young age.

Plate 8.1. St Irene Stefani 'Nyaatha'.
Public domain.

Aurelia became a member of the Consolation Missionary Sisters in 1911, taking the name Irene (meaning Peace) and was sent to Kenya as a missionary in January 1915 to work as a nurse. The local people gave her the name "Nyaatha" ("mother of mercy"). During World War I she nursed the wounded in military and civilian hospitals in Kenya and Tanzania. After the war she helped establish a local congregation known as The Mary Immaculate Sisters and was then appointed to Our Lady of Divine Providence mission at Gikondi. She was the Superior of the Consolation Missionary sisters for eight years.

> An eye-witness said: *"Nyaatha was kind to children and the sick. She used to ride a horse that she would tether to a croton tree near our house. She taught us how to pray in Latin. She used to come to our house often because she was a close friend of my late father. She would bring us food, gifts, sweets and biscuits. She brought medicine for the sick while the rest of us were taught how to pray".*[49]

Sister Irene's dedication to tending the sick cost her her life as she contracted plague from one of her patients and died in 1930.

More than twenty years after her death the fruit of Sister Irene's ministry became obvious. This was during the Mau Mau uprising in Kenya.

In Kenya, in the 1950s the Mau Mau movement developed within the Kikuyu tribe based upon legtitimate grievances over segregated education, land and unequal pay between white and black employees.[50] It was revolutionary, nationalistic, anti-colonial and anti-Christian. The Mau Mau terrorisd the British, killing sixty-three white famers on their properties.[51] The British army fought back and killed 11,000 people. The Mau Mau killed about 2,000 and coerced others into swearing the Mau Mau oath.[52]

> *"I swear that I will renounce Christianity and take up once more my name of Kikuyu. I swear I will never again approach missionaries, go to church or participate in the sacraments. I swear that I will combat the government in every possible way".*

Many Anglicans (mainly new converts) were martyred as well as seventy-five Catholics who also refused to swear and were martyred. The Blessed Irene Stefani Nyaatha, who baptised and/or evangelised them, was beatified by the Pope on May 23, 2015.[53] Although she had died in 1930 her converts were still holding strong.

Chapter 9
Wang Zhiming (1907-1973)

Wang Zhiming was born in 1907 in Wuding County, Yunnan Province, China, where he lived and died. By race he was a Miao, not Han-Chinese.

In 1906 missionaries Samuel Pollard, Arthur G. Nicholls, George E. Metcalf and Gladstone Porteous had come to work in Yunnan Province where their mission was so successful that forty years later about 130,0000 people had become Christians.

Christian schools had been established, which Wang attended before becoming a teacher. He was active in church affairs and was ordained in 1951 and, when Arthur G. Nicholls retired, Wang took charge of that work.

When the Communist government introduced the Three Self Movement designed to bring the churches under government control Wang signed the Three Self Manifesto. When he refused to take part in public denunciation meetings, which he regarded as sinful, he was declared to be a counter revolutionary.

In 1966 the Cultural Revolution commenced with a reign of terror by the Red Guard that lasted for a decade. Every aspect of Chinese culture was attacked as archaic: its theatre, dress, literature, architecture, written language and religion. Christianity, in particular, was persecuted.

"When the Cultural Revolution came to Wuding, he (Wang) was known to be a critic of the atheistic campaign of local Red Guards. In May 1969 he and other members of his family were arrested".[54]

Plate 9.1.

Statue of Wang Zhiming.[55]

On December 29, 1973 Wang Zhiming was executed in a stadium before a crowd of 10,000 citizens of Wuding, many of whom were Christians. It was meant to terrify them into subservience to the Revolutionaries but had the opposite effect. Wuding had fewer than 3,000 in 1973, but seven years later that number had increased to 12,000: more than 1,000 new Christians every year and the number is still growing.

> *"The communists had done everything in their power to kill the Church. They had not only closed all the churches, arrested all the pastors and many lay Christians, but had resorted to killing those that they deemed unwilling to follow the party line..... Christians were beaten, starved, exiled, buried alive, and sentenced to years of slave labour".*[56]

A statue of Wang Zhiming has been placed, with those of nine other modern martyrs from across the world, above the Great West Door of Westminster

Abbey in London but his real memorial is the vibrant Christian work in the Church in Wuding County, China.

Chapter 10
Janani Luwum (1922-1977)

Janani Luwum was born in a small villlage in Uganda in 1922. He was able to attend teacher training college where he demonstrated excellent leadership and negotiating skills. In his mid twenties he met Jesus Christ through the East Africa Revival movement, after which he began to preach on street corners and in the market place. Eight years later he was ordained in the Anglican church. Twenty-one years later he was consecrated Bishop of Northern Uganda in a service that was attended by the Commander of the Armed d Forces: the notorious Idi Amin.

Plate 10.1. Archbishop Luwum. Public domain.

The bishop's wife, Mary Lawinyo, had been an orphan so care for orphans featured highly in the Bishop's reform agenda, along with establishing community development projects to assist the poor. He encouraged the clergy to be a voice for the voiceless and to challenge violence and injustice, just as he, himself, did.

Two years after Bishop Luwum's consecration Idi Amin staged a coup and seized control of Uganda, instituting a brutal and violent regime which featured abuses of human rights, murder and immense suffering.

"Under President Amin, all Asians in the country were expelled, the economy collapsed, inflation rose and thousands were brutally murdered".[57]

Five years after his consecration Bishop Luwum became Archbishop of a large area that included Uganda and Rwanda. He continued to address the abuses of the government and its officials so that President Amin, a Muslim, began to plot revenge.

On February 15, 1977, a radio announcement ordered Luwum, other bishops and senior civil servants to attend a "special event" in the capital. This turned out to be a show-trial which accused Luwum of plotting to overthrow the government. Archbishop Luwum was detained and the following morning it was announced that he and two senior government officials had died in a car crash. When the body was returned to his wife and their nine children evidence of fatal gunshots was found.

The Archbishop had been advised to flee the country but had he declined to leave his flock. Many in Uganda and elsewhere were strengthened in their life and witness by Archbishop Luwum's example and courage.

Chapter 11
William Donald McClure
(1906-1977)

William Donald McClure (called Don) was born in Blairsville, Pennsylvania, USA on 27/3/1906. He was the third of seven children born to Margaret McNaughter, a Classics professor, and Rev. Robert Elmer McClure, a Presbyterian minister who loved hunting and, as an old man, went on a big game hunt with his son.

Don earned a B.A. from Westminster College and became a teacher in Khartoum, Sudan, for one year in 1929. He returned to America to train for the ministry for three years and married Lyda Lake Bell in 1932. He graduated with a B.D. from Pittsburgh Theological Seminary and was ordained in the United Presbyterian Church in 1934.[58]

Don and Lyda returned to the South of Sudan to work with the Shulla people in a land of wild animals.[59] There he was a 'jack of all trades and a master of none' and he devised the plan that a team of professionals working together for a few years would achieve more in church planting, leadership development and discipleship than the usual thin spread of missionary families was achieving.

Plate 11.1. Don McClure.

Public domain.

In 1938, the McClures initiated a new work among the Anuak people who lived on both sides of the Sudan-Ethiopian border. Because the Italians had captured Ethiopia, Don had to work on the Sudan side of the border. He established a mission station for only $1,000 using local materials, except for the mesh on the windows.[60] The work was interrupted by World War II but the mission was successfully established so that the McClures could move on by 1950.

In 1947, Rev. Dr. W. D. McClure was awarded a D.D. from Westminster College.

Their new work, from 1950, was with the Anuak people on the Ethiopian side of the border, at Akobo and Pokwo. In 1954 Don published an autobiographical account: *Red-Headed, Rash and Religious.*[61] After the gospel had been preached in every Anuak village there was at least one Christian in every village, the New Testament was printed in their language and ten percent of people were literate. The mission was almost self-sustaining so the McClures prepared to move on: to Gilo River.

By 1960 Don was pioneering this new work at Gilo River. His first job was to cut an airstrip out of the forest. He began to appeal to young Americans to give a year of service to the mission as volunteers and his daughter Lyda and his son, Don Jr., volunteered. Two years later a local Anuak pastor took over the work.

In 1962 Don became the General Secretary of the American Presbyterian Mission based in Addis Ababa: a desk job for an active wild game hunter, but he was fifty-seven years old and the mission would compulsorily retire him soon. Because of his work with the United Nations Committee of Refugee Relief, Don was regarded as an enemy of the Sudanese regime.[62]

The desert area to the South of Ethiopia, near the borders with Somali, Eritrea and Sudan, was a poor area and Gode was so near the border that Somali raiders and thieves often invaded as piracy and robbery were their only means of livelihood.[63] The Ethiopian government planned to pacify the area by building a model city at Gode, and Emperor Haile Silasse I of Ethiopia personally asked Don McClure and his Presbyterian Church to supervise the educational and medical work in this planned city. While he was living in exile (during the Italian occupation of Ethiopia) the Emperor had observed such services in Britain and upon his restoration to the throne was determined to modernise his country.

The Mission was slow to respond but Rev. Don McClure felt obliged to do so. In order to get the project underway, he retired from his mission in 1970 and became independent, depending on private funding. By 1977 the security situation had deteriorated quickly because of the civil war and all missionaries who had not been taken hostage were being evacuated. Don and his son, Don Jr flew to the Gode mission to hand it over to World Vision, whose staff members were already living there, including Graeme Smith and his family.

Guerilla fighters attacked and ransacked the compound one Sunday night. They took Don and Don Jr and Graeme Smith outside and, despite their pleas, the order to shoot was given. Rev. Dr Don McClure fell dead and his son fell but lay as if dead until the bandits had gone. The Missionary Aviation Fellowship plane arrived too late to save the old warrior of the Lord but all of the others were taken to safety.[64] His tombstone, set up in Gode by his grandson, Jonathan Partee, reads *"He who does the will of God lives forever."* William Don McClure was a remarkable pioneer missionary who gave fifty years of his life for the Kingdom of Jesus Christ, and a martyr who gave his all.

Chapter 12
Graham Staines (1941-1999)

Graham Staines was born in Palmwood, on the Sunshine Coast of Queensland, Australia, during World War II. As a teenager, he was very intelligent and studious, a devout Christian, who was so moved by the plight of people with leprosy that, when he saw a photograph of an Indian boy with leprosy named Josia Soren, *"he was filled with sorrow and compassion for those suffering from leprosy"* and resolved to live in India and help them.

Graham had helped to support his family in Australia by working in the office of a garage and learning accountancy at night school but he clung on to his calling. He lived and died for this purpose and his two sons, Philip (9) and Timothy (7) died with him. Gloria (later Staines) had arrived in India in 1981 so she had worked in India for eighteen years. They had been married for sixteen years. Mrs Staines and her only daughter, Esther, had not been with Graham and the young boys on the night of the tragedy.

Graham was sometimes referred to as Dr Staines because, with the availability of anti-biotic medication, he was able to cure people of leprosy. Graham was fifty-eight years old and had been working in Orissa for thirty-four years when he was martyred by Hindu extremists, led by Dara Singh, the leader of a nationalist gang. Graham and Gloria worked with an Australian mission EMSM (the Evangelical Missionary Society of Mayurbhanj). Graham ran the site in Baripada, which included the leprosy hospital and a farm for rehabilitating patients, which included dairy cattle. Graham spoke three languages including Oriya, the local tribal language, and he was well liked by the people who called him 'Saibo'.

One activity of the Mission was to run annual bush camps. On the night of one of these camps Graham and his boys were sleeping in their vehicle when they were attacked by a frenzied mob of from fifty to one hundred people. At the trial of Dara Singh, another accused man, Mahendra Hembram claimed that he, himself, was completely responsible but an eyewitness gave evidence that Dara Singh had torched the car, after an accelerant had been poured over it. When the Australian trio had tried to escape from the car they were pushed back in by people chanting the name of the nationalist party of the Prime Minister, Atal Behari Vajpayee, known as the BJP. They were obviously Hindu nationalists although the attack was condemned by the BJP. This tragic event was one element in a spate of attacks on Christians and churches, both before and after these killings.[65]

Although Mrs Gloria Staines appealed for clemency, Dara Singh was sentenced to death and twelve others were sentenced to life imprisonment. Two years later, when Gloria had left Indian, the death sentence was commuted to a life sentence and his twelve co-accused were acquitted by the High Court of Orissa. Mrs Staines returned to her work at the mission in June, 2006, but she urged reconciliation, telling a reporter,

"In forgiveness, there is no bitterness and when there is no bitterness, there is hope. This consolation comes from Jesus Christ".[66]

Plate 12.1. The Staines family. Wikipics.

In 2005 Mrs Gloria Staines was awarded the Padma Shrl by India for her work with leprosy patients. On January 23, 2020 *The Times of India* newspaper contained an article by Manati Singha, '21 years on Odisha village still weeps for Graham Staines'. A book was written about the tragedy: *Burnt Alive. The Staines and the God they Loved* (Gospel Literature Source) and two movies have been made.

Chapter 13
Martyred Priests of East Timor
(d.1999)

In 1999 a referendum was held in Timor Leste, the eastern half of a very poor island lying to the near North of Australia but South-West of Papua New Guinea, to decide whether the East Timor should remain under Indonesian control or should be granted independence.

East Timor was a Portuguese colony from 1702 to World War II. Allied forces occupied it to prevent a Japanese invasion but they were unable to prevent a Japanese conquest in 1942, during which time there was a severe famine and enormous loss of life on all sides. After the war Portugal returned to pick up where it had left off but the local revolutionaries, called Fretilin, engaged in guerrilla warfare for twenty years and drove them out in 1974. Very promptly, in 1975, Indonesia invaded and Fretilin was unable to prevail. Gough Whitlam was Prime Minister of Australia in 1975 and his government had not objected to Indonesia's conquest of the tiny, defenceless country, which is Australia's nearest neighbour. Timor Leste's people are Roman Catholic and Indonesia is largely Muslim (except for the island of Bali) and was becoming increasingly radical due to money and pressure coming from certain parts of the Middle East. Therefore it was a bad fit, moreover Indonesia was a brutal colonial power and world opinion had turned against its rule.

Plate 13.1. Suai, Timor Leste, c.1969. Public Domain.

International observers and Australian troops were overseeing the referendum but Indonesian troops did not attack. The result of the referendum - independence - was announced on September 4, 1999. The Indonesian troops, their supporters and local militiamen all reacted very negatively to this result. There was widespread violence, burning and looting. The capital, Dili, lay in ruins as though a cyclone had hit. Indonesian forces were reluctant to withdraw and did so slowly but when they did so they adopted a 'scorched earth policy' and the United Nations was forced to step in, permitting an INTERFET force to move in. It consisted mainly of Australian military, led by a future Governor General, Peter Cosgrove. It preserved order, but not until many people had been killed and the economy destroyed.

Everyone expected that Indonesians and pro-Indonesians would take revenge on those who had voted and many fled to the churches for safety. Four Roman Catholic priests were martyred. Three were shot trying to protect the refugees who were sheltering in church compound at Suai. They were Jesuit priest Rev. Tarcisius Dewanto (34) as well as Rev. Hilario Madeira and Rev. Francisco Soares who were shot at their church in Suai on September 6, 1999. Three hand grenades were then thrown in. The priests' bodies were found 20 km away, buried with 23 other people. There had been 2,000 refugees in the courtyard.[67]

Plate 13.2.1 Ruined Church and Compound at Suai.

A former classmate and friend reported of Father Dewanto's decision:

"As a pastor, he did not flee for safety, because the refugees sheltering in the church needed his encouragement".[68]

Then, on the night of September 11, Father Karl Albrecht Karim Arbie (70), who was the director of Jesuit Refugee Services in East Timor, was shot dead at the Jesuit-run refugee centre in the capital, Dili. He was buried with his fellow Jesuit.

"Where sin increases, grace incresases all the more" (Rom.5:20).

Chapter 14
Paulos Faraj Rahho (1942-2008)

In recent centuries the ancient Christian churches of the East have become scapegoats for such failed policies of the Western powers as the US invasion of Iraq in 2003 known as 'shock and Awe'. Clergy have been kidnapped and churches in Iraq and Syria have been destroyed since that invasion and the Chaldean Catholic Archbishop, Paulos Faraj Rahho of Mosul (in Iraq), was murdered in 2008. At that date only 3% of Iraq's population was Christian. The Chaldeans, who practise an ancient Eastern rite and are in Communion with Rome, are the most numerous Christian community.[69]

Some observers say that the Iraqi Church is growing under wartime conditions[70] but Anglican cleric Canon Andrew White ('the Vicar of Baghdad') recently said that Iraq was once *"the cradle of Christianity,"* but churches, manuscripts and artefacts are being wiped out.[71] Andrew White's congregation at St George's Cathedral was the only Anglican congregation in Baghdad but they all fled with thousands of other refugees to a camp in Jordan, although since then some have been relocated overseas and some have returned home. They are mainly widows with children and they are cared for and educated by foreign donors.

Archbishop Paul/Paulos Rahho was born during World War II (1942) in a small village near Mosul to a Chaldean Catholic family which had its roots in the ancient church of the East. From the age of 12 he studied at St Peter's junior seminary in Baghdad and graduated from the major/senior seminary at age 18. He was ordained a priest on June 10, 1965 (aged 23) and worked briefly in Baghdad before being appointed to St Isaiah's church in Mosul.[72]

In 1974 Rahho was sent abroad to the Pontifical University of St Thomas Aquinas in Rome from which he graduated with a Licentiate in Theology in 1976. As he had not chosen to marry he was eligible for the episcopate.[73] He was consecrated archbishop in 2001.

Archbishop Paulos Rahho built an orphanage for disabled children and built a bishop's residence. He founded and built the church of the Sacred Heart in Tel Keppe/Telkif, twelve miles (20km) north of Mosul, which the people call the Holy Spirit Church. In 2004 Rahho was frogmarched out of his residence and forced to watch it being burned down. Largely because he had tried to promote good relations with local Muslims, an imam offered him accommodation at his mosque.[74]

The new Archbishop was a humble and compassionate man and was famous for telling jokes. He was courageous and ready to confront evil and he once told the press that after Constantine the Great persecution ended in the West but not in the East adding *"even today we continue to be a church of martyrs"*.[75]

In June 2005 the Syrian Catholic Archbishop of Mosul, Basil George Casmoussa, was abducted at gunpoint but released after twenty-four hours. In 2007 the Chaldean parish priest of the Church of the Holy Spirit in Mosul, Father Ragheed Ganni, along with three deacons, were killed by an armed group.[76] Christian intellectuals, professionals and clergy had been targeted and about 300,000 Christians had emmigrated, which was the result the terrorists wanted.

Plate 14.1. Archbishop Rahho, martyr. Wikicommons.

In February 2008 Archbishop Paulos was ambushed and kidnapped. His driver and two bodyguards were killed. From the trunk (boot) of his captors' car he had used his mobile phone to tell his flock not to pay ransom for him. The demands were $3million, the release of Arab detainees and that Christians would join the fight against the Americans in a Christian militia.[77] The Archbishop had such health issues that he may have died but relatives reported seeing gunshot wounds. He had been buried in a shallow grave but was exhumed for examination and a ceremonial Christian burial.

Al Qaeda was found to be responsibe, one in particular was to be publicly executed, although the Church appealed for mercy.

The Archbishop well-knew the dangers he and his people were facing but they continued to carry the light of Jesus Christ in a dark place with courage and forgiveness.

Chapter 15
Conclusions

In every era of Christianity there have been martyrs, ever since John the Baptist and St Stephen the Deacon were martyred in the 1st Century. From then until the 4th century there were thousands killed for their resolute (some say stubborn) embrace of belief in Jesus of Nazareth as the Christ or Messiah.

One book that has been read for centuries is a collection of martyr stories so it is a genre of Christian literature that is evergreen. I refer to Fox's *Book of Martyrs* which was written by George Fox, the founder of the Quakers, who came very close to becoming a martyr himself, so great was the persecution of the movement in his lifetime. Their names should not be forgotten; nor their faith and deeds disregarded.

> *(Some) were tortured and refused to be released, so that they might gain a better resurrection. Some faced jeers and floggings, while still others were chained and put in prison. They were stoned, they were sawed in two, they were put to death by the sword. They went about in sheepskins and goatskins, destitute, persecuted and ill treated – the world was not worthy of them. They wandered in deserts and mountains and in caves and holes in the ground. They were all commended for their faith...* (Heb. 11:35bff)

Each of the Christians discussed above knew that the course they were taking was more dangerous than staying home and doing nothing yet they chose the path of discomfort and danger with courage and faith. These are not stories of the distant past but of our era and, even now, martyrs continued to give their lives for the good of the people to whom they minister and the cause of the Kingdom of Jesus Christ, saying with St. Paul:

"for to me to live is Christ and to die is gain" (Phil. 1:21).

BIBLIOGRAPHY

Primary Sources
Holy Bible, New International Version
(London: Hodder and Stoughton, 1978).

Reference Works
Moss, Denis, Simon Harding (ed), *Australian Christian Martyrs.*
Cross, F. L. & E. A. Livingstone (eds), *Oxford Dictionary of the Christian Church,*
(London: Oxford University Press, 1958-1972).
Anderson, Gerald, *Biographical Dictionary of Christian Missions*
(N.Y.: Simon & Schuster, 1998).
England, John C., *Asian Christian Theologies: Northeast Asia*
(2004).

Media Articles: Newspapers, Radio, Television
Anglican Communion News Service (ACNS) January 12, 2015, 'The Uganda Martyrs of Namugongo – the full truth behind this historic event', by Arfthur Matsiko,
https://www.google.com.au/search?q-the+uganda+martyrs+of+thamugongo
Anglican Focus, 'Ugandan Anglican Martyr Archbishop Janani Luwum' https://anglicanfocus.org-au/2020/05/29/ugandan-anglican-marttyr-archbishop-janani-luwum/
Aswat Al-Iraq (*Voices of Iraq*), 'Archbishop's kidnappers demand to form Christian militia'.
Sydney Morning Herald 13/8/2005, 'Last words from God's soldiers', by Alan Ramsey
Padre Arthur Bett (Assistant-Chaplain Gerneral), "Among the Ruins", Project Canterbury
The Age, 4/11/2008, 'Global Outcry at death of Iraqi archbishop', by Philip Pullella, Rome, and Aseel Kami, Baghdad,

www.theage.com.au/news/world/gobal-outcry-at-death-of-iraqi-archbishop/2008/03/14/1205472082065.html

The Times, 14/3/2008, 'Obituary of Archbishop Paul Farajk Rahho.'

The Guardian, 1/4/2020, 'Archbishop Paulos Faraj Rahho, Brave Iraqi Christian leader determined to stand with the flock', by Anthony O'Mahony.

https://www.theguardian.com/world/2008/apr/01/catholicism,[1] religion

The Kenya Standard, 6/1/2020, 'Witness to nun's kindness celebrates 100th birthday', by Jacinta Mutura.

https://www.standardmedia.co.ke/central/article/2001355455/witness-to-nun-s-kindnerss-celebrates-100th-birthday

UAC News May 17, 2000, "Priestr 'Martyrs' of East Timor".

Uganda National Media, 'The valley that witnessesd Bishop Hannington's death' editorial@ug.nationalmedia.com

http://www.monitor.co.ug/artsculture/Reviews/The-valley-that-witnessed-Bishop-Hannington-s-death/691232-1411440-f5po0iz/indix.html

Secondary Sources

Hamlin, Dr Catherine, with John Little, *The Hospital by the River*
(Pan Macmillan, 201/204).

Huizenga, Lee Sjoerds, *John and Betty Stam: Martyrs*
(Zondervan, 1935).

Kauffman, Paul, *Fire on the Rim*
(Chichester, UK: Sovereign World, 1990).

Kinnear, Angus, *Against the Tide*
(Kingsway Publications, 1974).

Koehler, Ludmila, *Saint Elizabeth the New Martyr*
(N.Y.: The Orthodox Palestine Society, USA, 1988).

Langmore, Diane, *Missionary Lives: Papua, 1874-1914*
(1989).

McClure, W. Don, *Red-Headed, Rash and Religious*
(Indiana, PA: AG Haldin Publishing Co., 1954).

Partee, Charles, *Adventure in Africa: The story of Don McClure*

---

1.   https://www.theguardian.com/world/2008/apr/01/catholicius,m

(Grand Rapids: Zondervan, 1990).
Reed, Colin, *Walking in the Light*
(Brunswick East, Vic.: Acorn Press, 2007).
Woodbridge, John D. (ed.), *Ambassadors for Christ*
(Moody Press, 1994).

On Line Sources

Auntyfaith, 'The Biography of John and Betty Stam – Martyred Missionaries to China,'
https://auntyfaith.com/2019/09/15/the-biography-of-john-and-betty-stam-martyred-missionaries-to-china

Chander, Dr Ernest, 'A Rememberance and a Eulogy Dr Kenneth Scott, 6 Nov., 2014', https://folus_wordpress.com/2014/11/06/dr-kenneth-scott-a-personal-eulogy-by-dr-ernest-chander/

Dunn, Gordon, 'The Martyrdom of John and Betty Stam',
https:/omf.org/us/the-martyrdom-of-john-and-betty-stam/

'Elizabeth the New Martyr',
https://orthodoxwiki.org/Elizabeth_the_new_martyr

Find A Grave,'Elizabeth Alden "Betty" Scott Stam',
https://www.findagrave.com/memorial/6615052B7elizabeth-alden-stam/

Gorilla Safaris, 'About Bishop James Hannington'
https://www.mjsafarisuganda.com/about-bishop-hannington/

Hall, Michael, 'Kokoda Campaign – Sister May Hayman,
https://www.library.act.gov.au

Hovhannisvan, Hasmik, 'Bodil Bjorn – An Unsung Hero',
https://nefq.am/en/article/27216

Ihunnia, Daniel O., MSP, 'How Africa is Changing the Face of Mission,'
https://sedosmission.org/article/how-africa-is-changing-the-face-of-mission[2]

Kiefer, James E., 'James Hannington and the Martyrs of Uganda 29 October, 1885.'
http://justus.anglican.org/resources/bio/278.html

---

2.   https://sedosmission.org/article/how0-africa-is-changing-the-face-of-mission

Lane, Gary and George Thomas, 'Vicar of Baghdad Says Christianity is 'Over' in Iraq.'

http://www1.cbn.com/cbnnews/cwn/2017/march/vicar-of-baghdad-christianity-is-over-in-iraq

'Martyrdom calls for Mau Mau Victims'

http://www.nation.co.uk/news/Martyrdom-calls-for-Mau-Mau-victims/1056-2965130-55885h/index.html

Metropolitan Anastassy,' The Holy New Martyr Grand Ducheses Elizabeth Feodorovna,

www.orthodox.cn/saint/duchesselizabeth.en.htm[3]

Murre-van den Berg, Helen, 'A brief history of Christianity in Iran.'

https://www.hlmvandenberg.me/2017/01/20-a-brief-history-of-christianity-in-iran/

Popham, Peter, for *Women of Christianity*: 'Hindu mob burns missionary and two young sons to death',

womenofchristianity.com/graham-staines-and-his-two-young-sons-burnt-alive-wife-forgives-unconditionally

Respeks Group, Monday, April 2, 2012, 'RG2011... Armenian children – victims of the Gernovide', by R. Parimala Rai.

https://respeksgroup.blogspot.com/2012/04/rg2011-armenian-children—victims-of_html

Staines, Gloria, 'I Forgive Completely Those Who Killed My Husband and Children,'

http://southasianconnection.com/articles/341/1/Gvraham-Staines-and-His-Two-Young-Sons-Buernt-Alive-wife-Forgives-Unconditionally/Page1.html

Warren, M. A., 'Introduction' on the New Guinea Martyrs.

---

3.   http://www.orthodox.cn/saint/duchesselizabeth.en.htm

[1] Gorilla Safaris, 'About Bishop James Hannington'
https://www.mjsafarisuganda.com/about-bishop-hannington/ [Accessed 8/8/2020].

[2] Colin Reed, *Walking in the Light* (Brunswick East, Vic.: Acorn Press, 2007), pp. 42-43.

[3] Arthur Matsiko, 'The Uganda Martyrs of Namugongo – the full truth behind this historic event'
Anglican Communion News Service (ACNS) January 12, 2015.
https://www.google.com.au/search?q-the+uganda+martyrs+of+thamugongo   [Accessed 10/10/2017].

[4] Reed, *Walking in the Light, op.cit.*, p. 42.

[5] James E. Kiefer, 'James Hannington and the Martyrs of Uganda 29 October, 1885.'
http://justus.anglican.org/resources/bio/278.html [Accessed 10/10/2017.]

[6] Gorilla safaris, *op.cit.*, online.

[7] *Ibid.*

[8] 'The valley that witnessesd Bishop Hannington's death' editorial@ug.nationalmedia.com
http://www.monitor.co.ug/artsculture/Reviews/The-valley-that-witnessed-Bishop-Hannington-s-death/691232-1411440-f5po0iz/indix.html [Accessed 10/10/2017].

[9] Reed, *Walking in the Light, op.cit.*, p. 42.

[10] *Ibid.*

[11] Daniel O. Ihunnia, MSP, 'How Africa is Changing the Face of Mission,'
https://sedosmission.org/article/how-africa-is-changing-the-face-of-mission[4] [Accessed 21/12/'17].

[12] Gorilla Safaris, *op.cit.*, online.

[13] Hasmik Hovhannisvan, 'Bodil Bjorn – An Unsung Hero,'
https://nefq.am/en/article/27216 [Accessed 8/8/2020].

[14] Respeks Group, Monday, April 2, 2012, 'RG2011... Armenian children – victims of the Gernovide,' by R. Parimala Rai. [Accessed 12/8/2020].
https://respeksgroup.blogspot.com/2012/04/rg2011-armenian-children—victims-of_html

[15] This photograph is licensed under the Creative Commons Attribution Share Alike 3.0 unported license by Angus Kinnear, *'Against the Tide'* (Kingsway Publications, 1974).

[16] *Ibid*, also including from 1895, 1896 and 1909..

[17] *Ibid.*

[18] *Ibid.*

[19] *Ibid.*

[20] Gomiedas Institute, Princeton, NJ, 2000. The diary was left in Turkey hidden in a trunk, untouched, until well after the war.

4.   https://sedosmission.org/article/how0-africa-is-changing-the-face-of-mission

[21] Ludmila Koehler, *Saint Elizabeth the New Martyr* (N.Y.: The Orthodox Palestine Society, USA, 1988), p. 12.

[22] F. L. Cross and E. A. Livingstone (eds), *Oxford Dictionary of the Christian Church* (*ODCC*) (London, 1958/1972), *s.v.*, Elizabeth, St., of Hungary (aka Elizabeth of Thuringia).

[23] 'Elizabeth the New Martyr',
https://orthodoxwiki.org/Elizabeth_the_new_martyr [Accessed 8/8/2020].

[24] *Ibid.*

[25] Koehler, *op.cit.*, p. 30.

[26] Metropolitan Anastassy,' The Holy New Martyr Grand Ducheses Elizabeth Feodorovna, www.orthodox.cn/saint/duchesselizabeth.en.htm[5] [Accessed 17/8/2020].

[27] *Ibid.*

[28] *Ibid.*

[29] 'Elizabeth the New Martyr', *op.cit.*, online.

[30] Will Norton Sr, 'Triumph in Death: John and Betty Stam', in John D. Woodbridge (ed.), *Ambassadors for Christ* (Moody Press, 1994), pp. 185-186.

[31] Auntyfaith, 'The Biography of John and Betty Stam – Martyred Missionaries to China,' https://auntyfaith.com/2019/09/15/the-biography-of-john-and-betty-stam-martyred-missionaries-to-china [Accessed 20/7/2020].

[32] Find A Grave,'Elizabeth Alden "Betty" Scott Stam', https://www.findagrave.com/memorial/6615052B7elizabeth-alden-stam/ [Accessed 17/7/2020].

[33] Gordon Dunn, 'The Martyrdom of John and Betty Stam', https:/omf.org/us/the-msaartyrdaom-of-john-and-betty-stam/ [Accessed 23/7/2020].

[34] Will Norton, Sr., 'Triumph in Death: John and Betty Stam', in Woodbridge (ed.), *op.cit.*, p. 190.

[35] Find A Grave, *op.cit.*, online.

[36] 'Letter to Cornelius Stam' January 8, 1935, enclosing a copy of John's last letter. https://bgcarchivesblog.files.wordpress.com/2019/11/letter-to-cornelius-stam

[37] Huizenga, Lee Sjoerds, *John and Betty Stam: Martyrs* (Zondervan, 1935), p. 69.

[38] Dr Ernest Chander, 'A Rememberance and a Eulogy Dr Kenneth Scott, 6 Nov., 2014', https://folus_wordpress.com/2014/11/06/dr-kenneth-scott-a-personal-eulogy-by-dr-ernest-chander/
[Accessed 7/7/2020].

[39] All Saints' Belmont, 'Papua New Guinea Martyrs', https://www.belmontanglican.org/papua-new-guinea-martyrs/[6] [Accessed 12/8/2020].

---

5.   http://www.orthodox.cn/saint/duchesselizabeth.en.htm

[40] M.A. Warren, 'Introduction' on the New Guinea Martyrs.

[41] Michael Hall, 'Kokoda Campaign – Sister May Hayman, https://www.library.act.gov.au [Accessed 12/8/2020].

[42] My mother-in-law nursed with Sr May Hayman in Dubbo and attended the same church.

[43] Hall, *op.cit.*, online.

[44] *Sydney Morning Herald* 13/8/2005, 'Last words from God's soldiers', by Alan Ramsey .

[45] Padre Arthur Bett (Assistant-Chaplain Gerneral), "Among the Ruins", Project Canterbury.

[46] Diane Langmore, *Missionary Lives: Papua, 1874-1914* (1989)

[47] Denis Moss, Simon Harding (ed), *Australian Christian Martyrs.*

[48] *Ibid.*

[49] *The Kenya Standard*, 6/1/2020, 'Witness to nun's kindness celebrates 100th birthday', by Jacinta Mutura. https://www.standardmedia.co.ke/central/article/2001355455/witness-to-nun-s-kindnerss-celebrates-100th-birthday [Accesses 20/8/2020].

[50] Reed, *Walking in the Light, op.cit.,* p. 166.

[51] *Ibid.*, p. 160.

[52] *Ibid.*

[53] 'Martyrdom calls for Mau Mau Victims' http://www.nation.co.uk/news/Martyrdom-calls-for-Mau-Mau-victims/1056-2965130-55885h/index.html [Accessed 10/10/2017].

[54] John C. England, *Asian Christian Theologies: Northeast Asia* (2004), s.v., Wang Zhiming (1907-1973).

[55] Creative commons attribution licensed 3.0. unported license.

[56] Paul Kauffman, *Fire on the Rim* (Chichester, UK: Sovereign World, 1990), p. 148.

[57] Anglican focus,'Ugandan Anglican Martyr Archbishop[Janani Luwum'{Accessed 6/6/2020]. https://anglicanfocus.org-au/2020/05/29/ugandan-anglican-marttyr-archbishop-janani-luwum/

[58] Gerald Anderson, *Biographical Dictionary of Christian Missions* (N.Y.: Simon & Schuster, 1998), p. 446.

[59] Charles Partee, *Adventure in Africa: The story of Don McClure* (Grand Rapids: Zondervan, 1990), pp. 329-400.

[60] *Ibid.*, pp. 141-142.

[61] W. Don McClure, *Red-Headed, Rash and Religious* (Indiana, PA: AG Haldin Publishing Co., 1954).

[62] *Ibid.*, p. 351. Note that before the creation of the nation of South Sudan, Sudan was (as now) a largely Muslim country.

[63] Dr Catherine Hamlin with John Little, *The Hospital by the River* (Pan Macmillan, 201/204), p. 108.

[64] Partee, *op.cit.*, p.13.

[65] Peter Popham, for Women of Christianity: 'Hindu mob burns missionary and two young sons to death', womenofchristianity.com/graham-staines-and-his-two-young-sons-burnt-alive-wife-forgives-unconditionally [Accessed 17/7/2020].

[66] Gloria Staines, 'I Forgive Completely Those Who Killed My Husband and Children,' http://southasianconnection.com/articles/341/1/Gvraham-Staines-and-His-Two-Young-Sons-Buernt-Alive-wife-Forgives-Unconditionally/Page1.html [Accessed 17/7/2020].

[67] *UAC* News May 17, 2000, "Priest 'Martyrs' of East Timor".

[68] *Ibid.*

[69] Philip Pullella, Rome, and Aseel Kami, Baghdad, 'Global Outcry at death of Iraqi archbishop.' www.theage.com.au/news/world/gobal-outcry-at-death-of-iraqi-archbishop/2008/03/14/1205472082065.html [Accessed 4/11/2017].

[70] Heleen Murre-van den Berg, 'A brief history of Christianity in Iran.' [Accessed 10/10/2017]. https://www.hlmvandenberg.me/2017/01/20-a-brief-history-of-christianity-in-iran/

[71] Gary Lane and George Thomas, 'Vicar of Baghdad Says Christianity is 'Over' in Iraq.' http://www1.cbn.com/cbnnews/cwn/2017/march/vicar-of-baghdad-christianity-is-over-in-iraq [Accessed 4/11/2017].

[72] *The Times*, 14/3/2008, Obituary of Archbishop Paul Farajk Rahho.

[73] *The Guardian*, 1/4/2020, 'Archbishop Paulos Faraj Rahho, Brave Iraqi Christian leader determined to stand with the flock', by Anthony O'Mahony. https://www.theguardian.com/world/2008/apr/01/catholicism,[7] religion [Accessed 12/8/2020].

[74] *Ibid*

[75] *Ibid.*

[76] *Ibid.*

[77] Aswat Al-Iraq (Voices of Iraq), 'Archbishop's kidnappers demand to form Christian militia

I

---

7.   https://www.theguardian.com/world/2008/apr/01/catholicius,m

Don't miss out!

Visit the website below and you can sign up to receive emails whenever Deslee Campbell publishes a new book. There's no charge and no obligation.

https://books2read.com/r/B-A-LSULB-ATYZE

BOOKS 2 READ

Connecting independent readers to independent writers.

Also by Deslee Campbell

Memorable Christians
Phoebe's Sister's: Women Leaders in Early Christianity
Phoebe's Sisters: Women Leaders in Early Christianity
Phoebe's Sisters : Women Leaders in Early Christianity
Bright Shining Lights of an Earlier Era
Shining Lights of the Reformation
Shining Lights of the Reformation
Remarkable Post-Reformation Christians
Remarkable Post-Reformation Christians
Remarkable Post-Reformation Christians
Modern Christian Martyrs
Modern Christian Martyrs
Modern Christian Martyrs
Christian Women We Should Remember
Great Christian Men We Have Forgotten
Great Christian Men We Have Forgotten
Great Christian Men We Have Forgotten
Christian Women Leaders of the 20th Century

Standalone
The Topkapi Beggar
Voices From The Silence
Why a Roman Emperor Rebuilt Jerusalem and Jerash
Why a Roman Emperor Rebuilt Jerusalem and Jerash

Stones, Walls and Watchmen
Mothers in Israel
Ecclesia a Long Journey to Tomorrow
St Paul's Olive Tree Metaphor

Watch for more at www.synagogueandchurch.com.

About the Author

About the Author

Dr Deslee Campbell, a retired educational psychologist and teacher, is a prolific writer of both fiction and works concerned with history, religion and archaeology. She is particularly interested in art, artefacts and architecture as pathways towards understanding the past. Her doctoral thesis from the University of Sydney is entitled "The Iconography of Women: A Study of Byzantium and the Byzantine-influenced Mediterranean, A.D. 395-1204."

Read more at https://www.youtube.com/@synagogueandchurch911.

www.ingramcontent.com/pod-product-compliance
Lightning Source LLC
Chambersburg PA
CBHW022001170726
47994CB00021B/1556